The Reluctant Dragon

AN ENTERTAINMENT

T0088401

for

narrator, soloists,
SATB chorus, & instrumental ensemble
(or piano)

Words by
DAVID GRANT

Music by
JOHN RUTTER

Oxford University Press
Music Department, Great Clarendon Street, Oxford OX2 6DP

PREFACE

The Reluctant Dragon, in its original form, is a children's story by Kenneth Grahame, first published in 1898 in a collection of his stories called *Dream Days.* On one level it is a charming tale about a dragon who prefers writing poetry to fighting; on another level it is an allegory about prejudice and reconciliation – a children's story for grown-ups, rather like the same author's *Wind in the Willows.*

This musical adaptation was originally written as an 'entertainment' for The King's Singers (six male voices) and the City of London Sinfonia to perform at a Christmas concert. The present published version, for four soloists, narrator and chorus, can either be performed as a concert piece or staged in various ways. Children can participate in the chorus, though some altos, tenors and basses are essential. The parts of St. George and the Dragon are intended for adult singers; the Boy is probably best sung by a boy soprano, though a female soprano or mezzo-soprano is certainly possible. The orchestral accompaniment is within the capacity of good teenage or amateur players; piano accompaniment would be adequate, with double-bass and drums if possible.

Note: Kenneth Grahame gave the story a Christmas setting. This is not, however, essential to the narrative and has been made optional here by means of alternative versions of one or two passages of the text, so that the piece may be performed at any time of year.

This piece was commissioned by Abbotsholme Arts Society with funds provided by East Midlands Arts.

INSTRUMENTATION

Keyboard 1 (Electric piano, or piano)
Keyboard 2 (Harpsichord, or piano)
Percussion 1 (Glockenspiel, vibraphone, fireman's bell)
Percussion 2 (Drum kit)
Strings (Minimum 4,3,2,2,1)

Full scores and instrumental parts are on hire.

Duration: 23 minutes

CAST

BOY	Soprano or mezzo-soprano
DRAGON	Tenor
ST. GEORGE	Baritone
VILLAGER	Baritone or bass
MASTER OF CEREMONIES (can double VILLAGER)	Speaking part
NARRATOR	Speaking part
CHORUS	S.A.T.B.

No. 1: PROLOGUE

(Narrator and Chorus)

Words by DAVID GRANT
Music by JOHN RUTTER

*NARRATOR: This is the story of a boy, a saint, and a dragon. It happened one Christmas-time† long ago, when the world was different, and there were more dragons about than there are nowadays;

*Narration is to start as soon as the first chord is played. It is timed to end shortly before the chorus entry.
†Alternative: "one winter's time".

© Oxford University Press 1985
Printed in Great Britain
OXFORD UNIVERSITY PRESS, MUSIC DEPARTMENT, GREAT CLARENDON STREET, OXFORD OX2 6DP
Photocopying this copyright material is ILLEGAL.

23
S.
mp legato
A.
There lived a shep - herd and his son all a - lone.
T.
B.
mp legato
unis.
p
Each day and ev - 'ry day
28
mp
Each day and ev - 'ry day
the shep-herd watched his sheep;
32
the boy sat read - ing
p
cresc.
and dream - ing:
mp
p
cresc.
cresc.

B TENORS and BASSES
37
mf unis.
Read - ing myths and le-gends of the won - ders of the world. Knights in shin-ing ar-mour bear-ing
mf
(+Drums)
SOPRANOS and ALTOS
40
mf
ban-ners all un - furled; Tales of elves and gob-lins and the spi - rits of the woods;
Hpschd.
43
cresc.
f
Mon-sters in the sea and mon-sters on the land, and dra - gons!
mf cresc.
mf
f
Str. trem.
cresc.
f

C Slower-rubato
47
p wistfully
How he longed to meet a real, fierce, fi - ery dra - gon!
p
A
p wistfully
p
p
accelerando
(♩ = c. 168)
rall. al fine
51
mf cresc.
f
sca - ly, tai - ly, green - bod - ied, red - eyed
cresc.
fire-breath-ing, fear-some, fa - bu-lous, fai- ry- tale,
mf cresc.
f
accelerando
(♩ = c. 168)
rall. al fine
cresc.
f
55
p
Lento
dra - gon.
(Narration to overlap with last chord)
p
Lento
2 Vlns.
p

No. 2: NARRATION

(overlapping with the last chord of No. 1)

NARRATOR: ... And sooner than expected his chance came. One night the shepherd came home all of a tremble.

'It's all up with me!' he exclaimed. 'Never more can I go up on them there downs! You know that cave up there?– well, I saw this *creature* sticking half way out of the cave — as big as four cart horses and all covered with shiny scales!'

The boy yawned. 'It's all right, father... don't you worry... it's only a dragon. He won't give us any trouble. I'll go up there and have a talk with him.'

So, after tea, he did.

(ATTACCA NO.3)

No. 3: CHORUS

SOPRANOS and ALTOS
mf
dra-gons breath-ing hard.
Up a - long the vil - lage street and
S.
A.
T.
B.
mf
down be - yond the inn:
At last his chance had come for real ad -
D. B. pizz.
A
unis.
mp
-ven - ture to be - gin.
Up a - cross the hill - side all
unis.
mp
A
Vlns.
p cresc.
mp
(D. B.)
(+Drums)

20
(ALL VOICES)
crisp and fro - sty white:
Down the wind - ing wood - land path the
24
mf
boy ran swift - ly through the night
To the se -
mf
27
- cret hi - ding place, the fear - some fi - ery dra - gon's lair;
What ad -

30
- ven - ture, what ex - cite - ment, feels like ma-gic in the air!
mp
Now at
Str.
Elec. Pno.
sf
p
34 B Allegro non troppo (𝅗𝅥 = c. 60)
T. and B.
last he'll know the an-swers to a ple - tho-ra of puz-zles: Does the dra-gon say his grace and such be -
Str.
37
SOPRANOS and ALTOS
ALL VOICES
- fore he chews and guz-zles? Does he use a ta - ble nap-kin or a knife and fork and spoon? Does he
40
accelerando
wash his claws and whis-kers care - f'ly when he dines at noon?

SOPRANOS and ALTOS
Più mosso
43
mf
C
When he tries to eat an ice-cream does his fi - ery breath-ing melt All the
Str. pizz. +Glock.
mp
46
TENORS and BASSES
ice and cream and send it trick-ling down his sca - ly pelt? If he sniffs at plants and flo-wers does he
rit.
a tempo
49
ALL VOICES
make the blos-soms droop? Does he singe his hair and whis-kers when he blows up - on his soup? By the
52
D
time the boy had reached the high-est point a-mong the hills He was dream-ing all of dra-gons and their

55
in-stant dam-sel grills: Do they kill be-fore they grill or do they like to hear the screams Of their
58
Meno mosso
f
gent-ly roast-ing vic-tims spit-ted right a-long their seams? And in case you all are think-ing that this
f
61
rall.
Lento (in 4)
S.
A.
pp
sub-ject's done to death—Well, don't wor-ry, we shall stop now 'cos we've all run out of breath.
T.
B.
pp
Segue No. 4
rall.
Lento (in 4)
f

No. 4:

(Boy, Dragon, St. George, Chorus)

NARRATOR: And sure enough, just outside a small but comfortable cave in the hillside, a dragon lay stretched out, purring contentedly. The boy approached....

10
brightening
(clears throat)
lack some-thing. . I'm a po-et, you see. Would you like to hear one of my ear-ly ef-forts?
pizz.
A Moderato con sentimento (♩ = 104)
14
mf
Huff, lit-tle dra-gon, thro' your lit-tle ba-by nos-trils, Huff, my lit-tle sca-ly one, and
mp
17
light pa-pa's ci-gar. Snort, lit-tle fel-low, with your lit-tle ba-by dra-gon snout,
20
Blow-ing steam-y bub-bles thro' your ho-ney in the jar.
Freely
f
enthusiastic
BOY
doubtful
What do you think? Well,

23
Slow (♩ = 60)
DRAGON
Freely
yes... Mind you, I al-so cul-ti-vate a more con-tem-p'ry style: Here's a pas-sage from my *Three Quin-*
sfp
Str. trem.
sfp
sfp
sfp
sffz
26
B a tempo (♩ = 60)
mf very intense
- tets:
Seeth - ing pitch and bet - ting slips
gliss.
sim.
p
pizz.
31
Doppio (♩. = 120)
Co - a - gu - late the bat-tle-ships....
But
sf
(S. Dr.)
sfp
f
35
CHORUS
(Villagers)
hark! What do I hear in the di - stance?
p
mf

39
C
S.
mp but aggressive
unis.
A.
We want the dra-gon! Scrag 'im, do 'im, chop 'is 'ead_ off! We want the dra-gon! Scrag 'im,
T.
B.
mp but aggressive
C
p
45
cresc.
spike 'im, cut 'is froat!_____ We got St. George and 'is 'orse and sword and
cresc.
froat! We got__ St. George, we got St. George
50
buck - ler; When St. George 'as done wiv 'im, 'E won't be worth__ a groat!____
55
mp
We want the dra - gon! 'E's bin plun - der - in' and pil - lag- in'! We want the
unis.
mf

60
f
unis.
dra-gon! 'E's bin scor-ching all the crops! St. George 'll spike the pe - ri - sher, the
div.
f
65
accel. ad lib.
aw - ful sca - ly ra - vi-sher; St. George 'll swoosh 'is great big sword and thump 'im round the chops!
D Same tempo (♩ = 120)
71
DRAGON
mf (pained)
O, how un - couth, how vul - gar! How un - ut - ter - ab - ly aw - ful!
D Same tempo (♩ = 120)
mp
75
And it does-n't ev-en rhyme! But who is this?
E
St. GEORGE
f
Saint George, at your
E Poco più mosso (♩ = 132)
f
(+S. D.)

80
Poco meno mosso (♩ = 120)
ser - vice! The hour of reck-'ning has come, sir! Nev-er more shall you wreak your
mf
84
ter - ror up - on these poor sim - ple folk! What wea - pons do you choose?
DRAGON
89
mp (quite faint at the thought)
Wea - pons, dear fel-low? None, dear boy!
cresc.
Can't fight, won't fight!
mf
A - ny-way—
p
cresc.
mf
93
St. GEORGE
f
Attacca No. 5
why must I be de - feat - ed? Be - cause it's in the sto - ry!
f

No. 5: TRIO

(St. George, Dragon, Boy)

14
I'm a lit - e - ra - ry dra - gon; Not a drop, not a drop of fight in me.
18 A
All my Sturm and Drang is pan - to - mime; I would-n't hurt a
21
fly. If you're going to cut up rough then I'll
24
poco rall.
a tempo
B
BOY
f
just sit down here and cry!
Stu - pid dra - gon! Can't you think of
mf
p
3

28
what a no - ble sight there'd be: Nos-trils flar - ing, scales a - flash - ing, ar - mour
32
St. GEORGE
mf risoluto
glint - ing, ban-ners wav - ing, don't you see? It's a case of King and Coun-try, do or
35
die, show the flag, With a gin and t. to brace you it - 'll soon be in the bag! Ev - 'ry
38
cresc.
chap with a - ny feel-ing feels a qui-v'ring of his lips, When the fight - ing is all ov - er and the
cresc.

11
BOY
C
f
Stu-pid dra - gon! Can't you think of
DRAGON
mf
Ar - my man - ual! Sto - ic pos - es!
f
mp
foe has had his chips. I say, old boy, look here, old chap, you've got to do your stuff, It's not
C
f
p
44
what a no - ble sight there'd be: Nos-trils flar - ing, scales a -
Stuff and non - sense! Don't you see? I'm a lit - e - ra - ry
Bri - tish, it's not puk-ka just to sit there in a huff; So pull your - self to - ge - ther, man, and
47
flash - ing, ar - mour glint-ing, ban-ners wav - ing, don't you see?
dra - gon; Not a drop, not a drop of fight in me.
mf
strike a sto - ic pose! I have read the Ar - my man-ual and I'll show you how it goes. It's a

50
O, the splen-dour, with all the shout - ing, cheer - ing
All my Sturm and Drang is pan - to - mime; I would-n't hurt a
case of King and Coun - try, do or die, show the flag, With a gin and t. to brace you it - 'll
53
throng! What a no - ble sight,
fly. If you're going to cut up rough then I'll
soon be in the bag! Ev - 'ry chap with a - ny feel - ing feels a qui-v'ring of his lips When the
56
rall.
mp dim.
what a no - ble sight, what a no - ble
mp
dim.
just sit down here and cry, yes I'll cry.
mp dim.
fight - ing is all ov - er and the foe has had his chips, when the foe has had his
rall.

59
a tempo
D
sight! But what shall we do?
But what shall we do? I've no wish to fight you.
chips. But what shall we do? And
a tempo
D
legato
64
So what shall we
frank-ly, old chap, I don't want to fight you ei - ther! So what shall we
68
Why don't you rig the fight?
do? Why don't we rig the
do? Why don't we rig the
Str. trem.

No. 6: TRIO and CHORUS

(Boy, Dragon, St. George, Chorus)

Fifties rock 'n roll style (♩ = 144)

ALL VOICES (CHORUS ONLY)

unis.

With a one and a two, with a one, a two, and

Elec. Pno.

D.B. pizz. +Drums

5
BOY
1. First he
S.
A.
mf
dim.
ov - er to you!
wop wop wop wop
T. unis.
B.
mf
dim.
Doo ba doo wop doo ba doo wop
mf
8
St.GEORGE
DRAGON
1. waves his spear a - round, Yes I wave my spear a-round, Ah! he waves his spear a-round; oh! how aes-
2. both be - gin to lunge, Good! we both be - gin to lunge, Nice! let's have a jol - ly lunge—so stim - u -
p
wop wop wop wop wop wop
p
Doo ba doo wop doo ba doo wop doo ba doo wop

11
BOY
St.GEORGE
DRAGON
- the - tic!
- la- ting!
Then his char-ger paws the ground, Yes, me char-ger paws the ground. Ah! his
Then he sticks you in the gut Wow! I stick him in the gut? What! he
1. aes-the-tic
2. - u - la - ting
wop wop wop wop
doo ba doo wop doo ba doo wop doo ba doo wop

14
BOY
St.GEORGE
char - ger paws the ground; my! how ath - le - tic!
sticks me: tut, tut, you nas - ty per-son!
Now you let him have a burst—Right, you
No, it's just a bag of tricks—Make it
wop wop
1. ath- le - tic
2. - sty per - son
Ooh
doo ba doo wop doo ba doo wop

17
1. Dragon
2. Boy
1.
BOY
let me have a burst,_ Oh! I'll give him quite a burst; how py - ro - tech-nic!_
look as though it sticks_ so the
2. Then you
ah
ooh
ah_____ -ro-tech - nic!_
1.
30
2.
DRAGON
A
crowd-'ll get their kicks. I hope you're cer - tain!_
ooh
ah
And now, young fel - low,___
f
f
2.
A

*or other scat syllables.

39
St. GEORGE
doo doo wop bi doo bi doo shoo bi doo ba da doo wa
Ba doo bi di
and now St. George!

12
BOY
doo doo doo wa a doot-'n-doo doo wa ba doot-'n doot-'n doo doo wa
Now you
doo wa doo doo wa doo doo wa doo wa doo wa Sec-ond half!

46
B Poco più mosso
St.GEORGE
DRAGON
speed it up from there:_ Feint and lunge and claw the air,_ Wave your sword all de-bon-air–I've got the
p
Wop bee doo dee wop bee doo bee wop bee doo bee
p
Doo bee doo bee doo bee doo bee doo bee doo bee doo bee doo bee doo bee
B Poco più mosso
3
49
BOY
St.GEORGE
DRAGON
feel - ing._ Make it na - sty, make it mean,_ Make it start to sort of seem_ Like we
f
He's got the feel - ing!_
p
Wop bee doo bee wop bee doo bee
f
doo He's got the feel - ing!_
p
doo bee doo bee doo bee doo bee doo bee doo bee
3

52
BOY
St.GEORGE
meant it—what a dream, O the e - mo - tion!
Then you screw it up to pitch Till the
wop bee doo bee O the e - mo - tion!
wop bee doo bee
doo bee doo bee doo bee doo O the e - mo - tion!
Doo bee doo bee doo bee

55
DRAGON
BOY
crowd be-gins to itch For a kill - ing, for a vic- to-ry, for cur - tains!
Yes, but
wop bee doo bee doo
for cur - tains!
doo bee doo bee doo bee doo

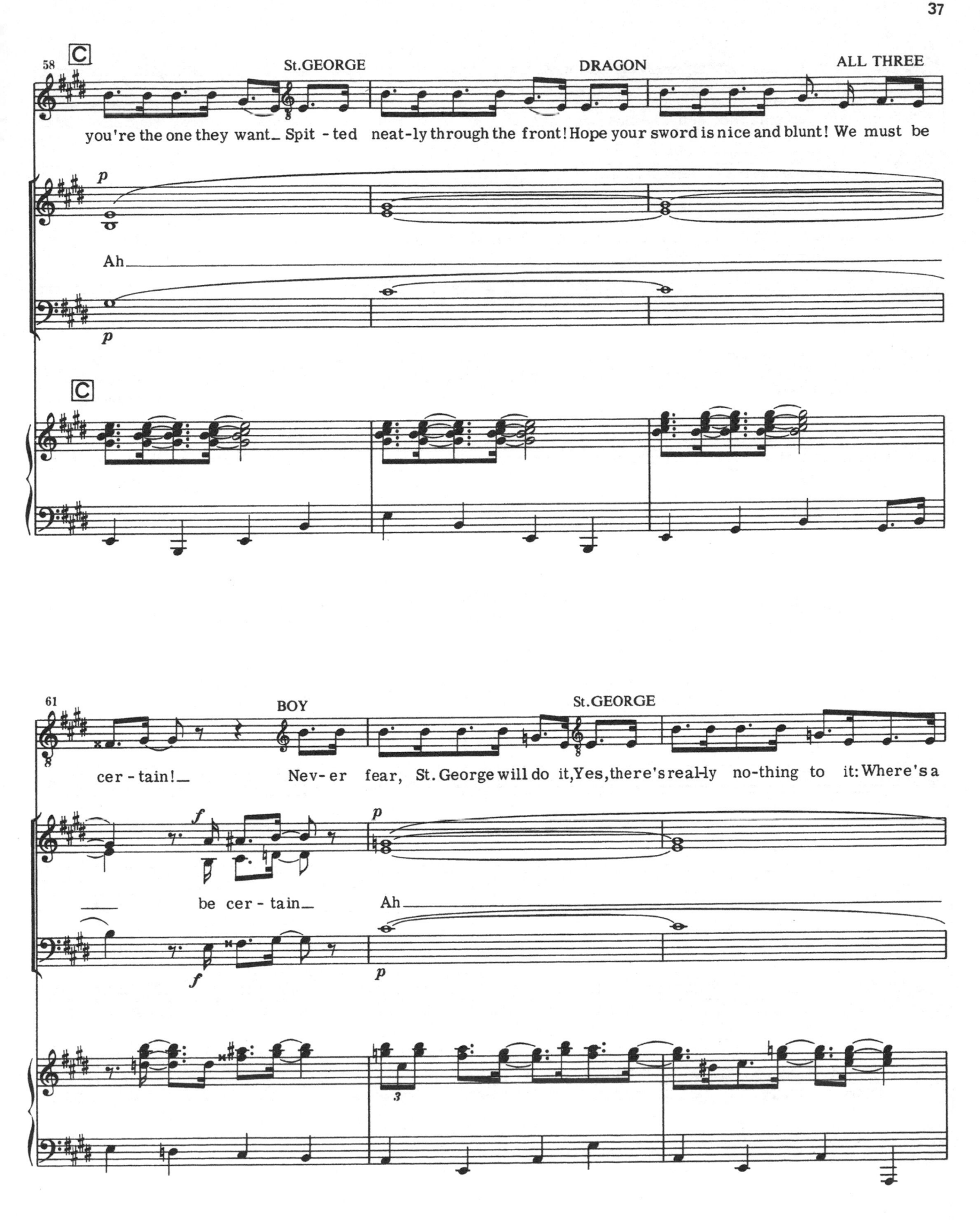
58
C
St.GEORGE
DRAGON
ALL THREE
you're the one they want_ Spit - ted neat-ly through the front! Hope your sword is nice and blunt! We must be
p
Ah
p
C
61
BOY
St.GEORGE
cer - tain!_ Nev- er fear, St. George will do it, Yes, there's real-ly no-thing to it: Where's a
f
p
be cer - tain_ Ah
f
p
3

64
DRAGON
bit of you with no sen-sa-tion in it? You could pin me in the wing: See, it's
-tion in it ah
67
BOY
real-ly on-ly skin, That's the place, St. G., so take it to the lim-it!
ooh ah the lim-it,

No. 7: TOURNAMENT

(Narrator, Master of Ceremonies, Boy, Dragon, St. George, Villager, Chorus)

NARRATOR: .... And not a moment too soon. Already it was time the tournament to begin, and a crowd of villagers had gathered.

6
unis.
'ead off! We want the dra-gon! Scrag 'im, spike 'im, cut 'is froat!
pp
Vc.
Cb.
MASTER OF CEREMONIES: Silence, pray silence, ladies and gentlemen! On my left, the fearsome, fiery dragon!
CHORUS: Boo! Hiss! Down with the dragon! (etc.)
MASTER OF CEREMONIES: And on my right, the fearless St. George!
CHORUS: Hooray! Bravo! Up St. George! (etc.)
11
sfz
mf cresc.
MASTER OF CEREMONIES: Right now, gentlemen, three rounds of good clean fiery combat, and may the best man win. On the word of command ..... charge!
18
Andante
pp
22
A
Lento
S.
p
accelerando poco a poco
A.
Clop clop clop clop clop clop clop clop clop clop clop clop
T.
B.
p
Clip clip clip clip clip clip clip clop clip clop clip clip clip clip

* like swords swishing through the air.

48
Presto
ff
fshoo fshoo fshoo fshoo fshoo fshoo fshoo Phew!
fshoo fshoo fshoo fshoo fshoo fshoo fshoo Phew!
ff Presto
Bell
clop clop clop clop clop fshoo fshoo fshoo fshoo Phew!
ff
clip clip clip clip clop fshoo fshoo fshoo fshoo Phew!
MASTER OF CEREMONIES: (before music restarts) Round 1: no hits; a draw!....
55 B Vivace
.... Round 2: take your marks ... charge!
S.
A.
p
Pat-ter pat-ter pat-ter pat-ter
T.
B.
Boom boom boom boom
B Vivace
p
61
St.GEORGE
f
Come, fi - ery fiend, your doom is seal -
pat-ter pat-ter pat-ter pat-ter boom
(p)
pat-ter pat-ter pat-ter pat-ter
boom thunk thunk thunk boom
boom boom boom thunk

66
DRAGON
f
-èd; Your fell ca-reer is at an end, sir! Seal on, you
pat-ter pat-ter pat-ter pat-ter pat-ter pat-ter pat-ter pat-ter boom
thunk thunk boom boom boom boom boom boom boom
71
a-ni-ma-ted scare-crow! Come let me roast you like a
pat-ter pat-ter pat-ter pat-ter pat-ter pat-ter pat-ter pat-ter pat-ter pat-ter
boom boom boom thunk thunk thunk boom boom boom boom
76
St.GEORGE
DRAGON
f
ca-pon! My sword your flame shall soon ex-tin-guish! It might if
pat-ter pat-ter thunk swish swish swish swish thunk
boom thunk thunk
81
St.GEORGE
DRAGON
p sub.
cresc.
you'd the strength to lift it, pu-trid pup-pet! Man-gy mon-ster! Fee-ble faint-heart-ed, fea-ther-brained
cresc.
thunk thunk swi-shthunk swi-shthunk swi-shthunk thunk
cresc.

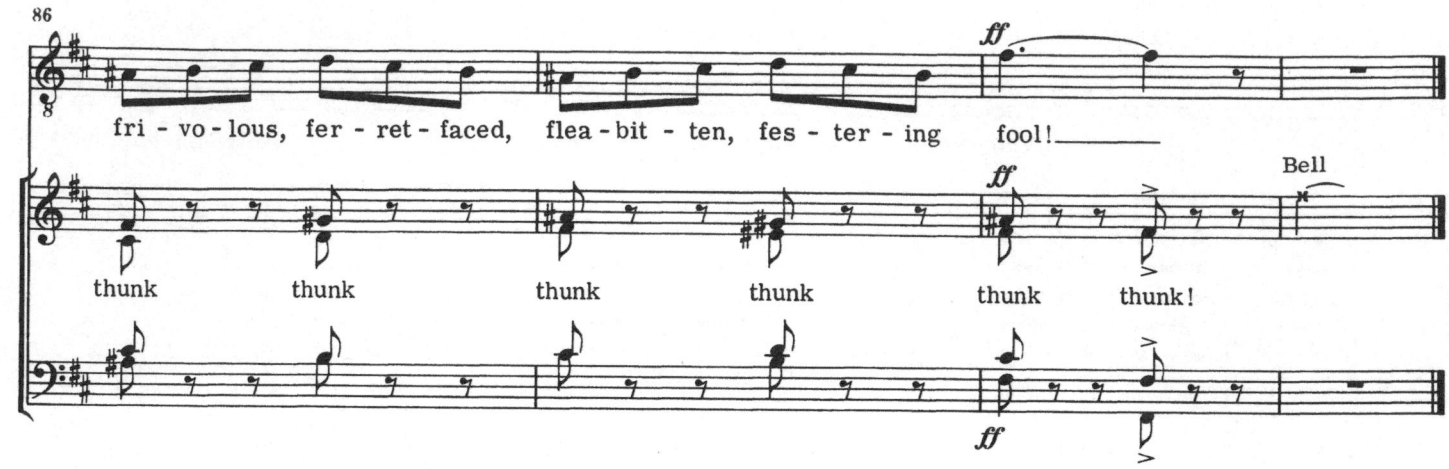

MASTER OF CEREMONIES: Round 2: Dragon wins on points!.....

101
pa pa pa pa pa pa pa pa
pa pa pa pa pa pa pa pa
mf
pat-ter boom pat-ter boom pat-ter boom
p
cresc.
pat-ter pat-ter pat-ter pat-ter
pat-ter boom pat-ter boom pat-ter boom pat-ter
Boom boom
105
f
pa pa pa pa pa pa pa pa pa
pa pa pa pa pa pa pa pa pa
pat-ter pat-ter pat-ter pat-ter clish boom
pat-ter pat-ter pat-ter pat-ter
boom pat-ter boom pat-ter clish boom
boom pat-ter boom pat-ter
boom boom clish boom thunk thunk boom boom
109
pa pa pa pa pa pa pa pa pa
pa pa pa pa pa pa pa pa pa
pat-ter pat-ter pat-ter pat-ter clish boom
(f)
clish thunk
boom pat-ter boom pat-ter clish boom
clish thunk
boom boom clish boom thunk thunk clish thunk

113
D
DRAGON
f (expiring groan)
dim.
mf
Aargh a - las, I
T.
thunk clish clish thunk urgh
p
B.1
thunk clish clish thunk urgh
p
B.2
thunk clish clish thunk urgh
p
D
p
120
die! A - las, I die!
p
T.
B.
mf
Hoo - ray!
St.
sim.

126
S. unis.
A.
Hoo - ray! St. George has van-quished the
George has van - quished the dra - gon!
131
E
BOY
p
dra - gon!
Oh, Dra - gon, are you real - ly hurt?
E
(p)
137
DRAGON
(loud stage whisper)
Not a scratch, dear boy, did- n't I do it well! Shush, they'll hear you! Just keep
f
BOY
mf
p
pizz.

NARRATOR: So that night there was a great banquet. I'm not certain if he was actually invited, but the dragon went along too, and even took some of his poetry, just in case anyone asked him to read a little of it. Everyone feasted and drank.....

*may be sung by MASTER OF CEREMONIES.

Attacca No. 8

No. 8: BANQUET FUGUE

(Chorus)

Lively, in 2 (𝅗𝅥 = c. 96)

5
mp
pep - per and the mus - tard and
TENORS mf
Guz - zle, guz - zle, guz - zle, munch, munch, gob - ble, gob - ble,
8
vi - ne - gar and the bread; the
chomp, Pass the salt and the pep - per and the mus - tard
BASSES mf
Guz - zle, guz - zle, guz - zle,
11
salt! Pass the salt and the pep - per and mus - tard and
mp
and vi - ne - gar and the
munch, munch, gob - ble, gob - ble chomp, Pass the salt and the pep - per and the

14
SOPRANOS
mf
Guz - zle, guz - zle, guz - zle,
bread.
Pass the salt
and
bread, pass the salt and the pep - per, the pep - per, the
mp
bread, pass the salt and the pep - per, the pep - per and
17
munch, munch, gob - ble, gob - ble, chomp, Pass the salt and the pep - per and the
pep - per.
pep - per and mus-tard and the vi - ne - gar and the
the mus - tard.
p
Guz - zle,

20
A
p (delicate)
bread. Munch, munch, munch, munch, gob-ble, gob-ble, gob - ble,
p (delicate)
Chomp, chomp, chomp, chomp,
p
bread. Gob-ble, gob - ble, gob - ble, gob-ble, gob-ble, gob-ble,
guz-zle, guz- zle, guz-zle, guz-zle, guz-zle, guz-zle,
A
p
23
munch
f
chomp, chomp, chomp, chomp, chomp, chomp,
f
munch, chomp, chomp, chomp, chomp, chomp, chomp,
f hearty
guz - zle, guz - zle, guz - zle, munch, munch, gob - ble, gob - ble, chomp, Pass the salt and the
f

26
B
f (outraged)
There's a fly in my
mf
chomp, chomp, gob - ble, gob - ble, chomp.
mf
chomp, chomp, chomp, chomp, chomp, chomp, chomp, chomp.
mf
pep - per and the mus - tard and the bread. Slurp, slurp, slurp,
B
mf
29
soup! There's a fly in my soup!
f (outraged)
There's a fly in my soup! There's a fly in my
slurp, slurp, slurp, slurp, slurp, slurp, slurp, slurp, slurp, slurp, slurp, slurp,

32
f
Fetch the doc - tor, I'm
f
Well, it won't drink much, Sir! Fetch the doc - tor, fetch the
mf
f
soup, in my soup! Fetch the doc - tor, fetch the doc - tor,
f
slurp, slurp, slurp, slurp, slurp. Fetch the doc - tor,
f
36
dim.
rall.
C a tempo
pp
feel - ing ra - ther strange.
dim.
pp
doc - tor, I'm feel - ing strange. Guz- zle, guz - zle, guz - zle,
dim.
pp
I'm feel - ing ra - ther strange.
dim.
pp
I'm feel - ing strange.
rall.
C a tempo
pp

39
cresc.
p
mp cresc.
guz-zle, guz-zle, guz-zle, guz-zle, chomp.
Guz-zle, guz- zle, guz - zle,
p
cresc.
mp cresc.
Guz-zle, guz-zle, guz - zle, chomp, chomp, chomp, chomp,
pp cresc.
mp cresc.
Guz-zle, guz-zle, guz - zle, munch, munch, gob-ble, gob-ble, chomp, chomp, chomp, chomp,
cresc.
p cresc.
mp cresc.
42
mf cresc.
f
Guz-zle, guz-zle, guz - zle, guz-zle, guz-zle, guz - zle, munch, munch, chomp,
mf cresc.
f
munch, munch, gob- ble, gob- ble, chomp, gob-ble, gob - ble, chomp, gob-ble, chomp,
mf cresc.
f
munch, gob- ble, chomp, gob-ble, chomp, gob-ble, gob - ble, chomp, munch, munch, gob-ble,
mf cresc.
f
munch, guz- zle, guz-zle, guz-zle, guz- zle, guz-zle, guz-zle, guz- zle, guz - zle, chomp,
mf cresc.
f

No. 9: FINALE

(Narrator, St. George, Chorus)

6
accel.
mp cresc.
I thought St. George had slain him once and for
dra-gon do-'in' 'ere?
mp cresc.
accel.
10
♩ = c. 152
ff
poco rall.
♩ = 132
St. GEORGE
f
all..... cut off his 'ead!
Cut off his head?
I can't do that!
ff
♩ = c. 152
f
Str. trem.
poco rall.
sfz
♩ = 132
mf
14
allargando
A Andante maestoso (♩ = 96)
f risoluto
He's a jol-ly good chap.
I'll give him a stern talk-ing-to: now
mf legato
poco marc.

poco rit.
a tempo (♩ = 96)
19
that should do the trick in - stead!
mp semplice espress.
Why don't we let
muted strings
dim.
p legato
23
by - gones be by - gones— turn a new leaf—make a - no- ther start?
poco rubato
Af-ter all,
27
Alternative version:
They won't harm you;
più dolce
dra-gons aren't so bad if you just get to know them a bit;
and be - sides,

31
rall.
Poco meno mosso (♩ = c. 92)
poco rall.
B a tempo
we could all be friends.
it's near - ly Christ - mas.....
pp
p legato sempre
(+Elec. Pno.)
36
SOPRANOS and ALTOS
p soft and gentle
TENORS and BASSES
p
1. So let's be-gin a - gain; try an - oth - er way. Let's be-gin a -
Hpschd.
Elec. pno., Vib.
Bass
sim.
41
ALL VOICES
mp
- gain; There's a bet - ter way: Rule a line and start once
(+Drums)
46
SOPRANOS and ALTOS
p
more, Learn-ing from what's gone be-fore; Let's be-gin a - gain,

50
S.
A.
T.
B.
mp
C
2. So can we get it right this time?
Let's find a way to start a - gain.
mp
C
Str.
mp
55
Pos - si - bly.
An-oth-er chance in sight?
Take things ea - si - ly.
60
mf
Is there time to care a - gain, Time to hope and share a - gain?
mf
mf

64
mp
Too late to try it out a - gain?
mp
Is it all too late?
mp
mp
68
D
unis.
p
Hum
unis.
p
3. The star-light in the skies and the moon - light;
D
p
delicately
72
(hum)
Hum
The fire-light in your eyes and the can - dle-light Ev-'ry crea-ture

77
Hum
soft - ly bless, Touch-ing each with ten - der-ness, Help-ing us to
81
Hum
see, To see a bet-ter way a-head.
8
86
unis. pp very gently
E
4. The man-tle of the night wraps things si - lent-ly: Noth - ing mor-tal
unis.
pp very gently
E
dim.
pp molto legato

91
poco cresc.
div.
mp
mf
shows; Let's step care - ful - ly. Make new tracks to - geth - er,
div.
poco cresc.
mp
mf
poco cresc.
mp cresc.
mf
96
mp
unis.
Walk hand in hand; And nev - er run and hide; The
mp
unis.
mp
100
cresc.
div.
f
mp
paths that we must tread lie side by side, The
div.
cresc.
f
mp
cresc.
f

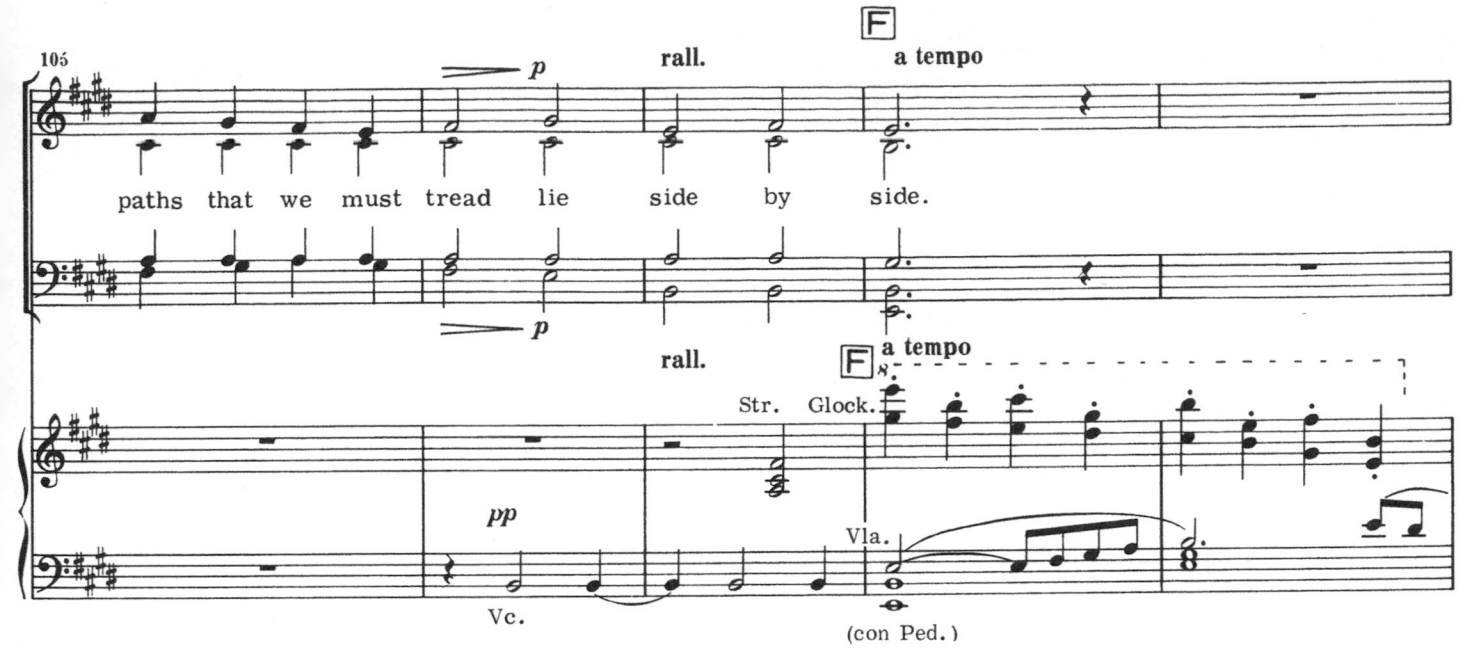

*NARRATOR: So at length the banquet ended. They set off up the hill arm in arm, the saint, the boy, and the dragon. The lights in the little village

began to go out; but there were stars, and a late moon, as they climbed the downs together. Soon they reached the top, and it was time for their ways to part.

They stood silent for a moment; then wished each other goodnight; and — a Merry Christmas. †

* Narration is to start during this bar. It is timed to end in the penultimate bar.
†Alternative text: "wished each other goodnight; and — sweet dreams".

Printed by Halstan